The Astrological guide to Hemp

The Astrological guide to Hemp

Matthew Edward Petchinsky

The Astrological Guide to Hemp: Stars, Signs, and Sacred Leaves
By: Matthew Petchinsky

Introduction

Cosmic Roots and Sacred Green

Since the beginning of human consciousness, we have turned our gaze skyward for meaning. The stars have served as maps for travelers, oracles for kings, and sacred symbols for seers. Equally, we have reached downward—into the soil—to find sustenance, medicine, and grounding. Hemp, one of the oldest cultivated plants known to humankind, exists as a powerful bridge between these two realms: the cosmic and the terrestrial.

This book is born from the understanding that astrology and hemp are not separate mystical domains, but intimately linked through energy, rhythm, and healing. Just as the moon pulls the tides and the sun rules the seasons, so too do the planetary influences shape our personalities, our physical well-being, and our spiritual evolution. Hemp, with its sacred versatility, responds to these celestial energies in profound ways—enhancing, balancing, and unlocking potential according to our zodiac blueprint.

Each chapter of this guide will dive deep into the vibrational essence of a zodiac sign and explore how hemp—through its many forms including flower, oil, fiber, smoke, and salve—can harmonize with your sign's ruling planet, elemental force, and energetic archetype. You'll discover that Aries thrives with activating, energizing hemp blends that spark action, while Pisces benefits from dream-enhancing hemp rituals that open the doorway to the subconscious. Taurus seeks comfort and luxury through hemp-infused foods and massages, while Gemini aligns best with smoke or tinctures that enhance clarity and expression.

But this book goes beyond personality traits. It is a spiritual map for working with hemp during astrological events such as full moons, new moons, planetary retrogrades, and solar returns. You'll learn how to harness the power of hemp during your personal moon sign's transit, how to craft rituals that align with Venus for love or Saturn for discipline, and how to create sacred moments with hemp that are in tune with cosmic shifts.

In a world rediscovering both the healing power of cannabis and the truth encoded in the stars, *The Astrological Guide to Hemp* is a timely fusion of the two. This is not a manual of medicinal science, nor a horoscope column with vague advice—it is a mystical and practical companion for those who want to root themselves in the earth while reaching for the divine.

Inside, you'll find:

- Rituals and meditations based on your sun, moon, and rising signs
- Alchemical correspondences between hemp, herbs, crystals, and astrological bodies
- Guides to using hemp for manifestation, rest, love, psychic vision, and grounding
- Seasonal and lunar timing charts for ritual optimization
- Sacred blends, teas, bath formulas, and sacred smoke combinations
- A cross-cultural and magickal respect for hemp as an ally—not a commodity

Whether you are a longtime astrologer, a spiritual seeker, a herbal enthusiast, or simply curious, this book invites you to explore your cosmic nature through the sacred green lens of hemp. Each leaf, each planet, each ritual speaks a language your soul already knows. May this journey reawaken that memory—and guide you toward harmony, healing, and cosmic alignment.

Welcome to the temple of the stars. The altar is set. The sacred leaf awaits.

Chapter 1 – Aries: The Ignition Leaf

The astrological year begins with Aries, the first spark of the zodiac—the sign of initiation, courage, combustion, and raw life force. Ruled by **Mars**, the planet of action and primal energy, Aries represents the birth of ambition, instinct, and momentum. In hemp alchemy, Aries is not content to sit still or drift in abstraction. Aries wants hemp to **energize, activate, and ignite**.

Hemp for Fire Energy: Energizing, Invigorating Blends

Hemp, when paired properly with Aries's fiery temperament, becomes a powerful ally in unleashing motivation, combatting fatigue, and sharpening one's inner drive. Aries thrives on momentum, but that momentum often burns fast and burns out. To balance this, we turn to **hemp-based blends** that combine **stimulating herbs** like **ginger, ginseng, yerba mate, or cayenne pepper** with **CBD-dominant hemp** to amplify energy while maintaining focus and reducing impulsivity.

These blends should **awaken the senses** and stimulate the **solar plexus chakra**, Aries's seat of willpower. Ideal delivery methods include **morning teas, aromatic oils rubbed on pressure points**, or **smoke blends** before physical exertion or a new venture. For Aries, hemp is not a sedative—it's a **sacred flame fuel**.

Sample Energizing Blend for Aries:

- Organic hemp flower (CBD-dominant)
- Dried ginger root
- Dried lemon peel
- Ginseng powder
- Pinch of crushed chili (for courage)

Steep as tea or grind for loose-leaf vaporization. Use at sunrise or before an ambitious task.

Best Uses: Infused Oils for Motivation, Teas for Stamina

Aries benefits greatly from **topical hemp-infused oils** designed for movement and goal-setting. These oils can be created with **coconut or jojoba oil**, infused with **rosemary, peppermint, and hemp**, then charged under a waxing moon in Aries. Rubbed onto the chest, shoulders, or the soles of the feet, this oil can invigorate the body and center the mind before action.

Teas, on the other hand, serve as an internal battery recharge. Aries often skips self-care or pushes too hard. A daily hemp tea ritual can nourish adrenal glands, reduce inflammation from overexertion, and ground their restlessness into sustainable effort.

Affirmation with Tea:

"With each sip, I ignite with purpose. I am ready, focused, and ablaze with sacred intention."

Mars-Ruled Rituals with Hemp Incense

Mars is not just about war—it is the archetype of **willpower, sexuality, survival, and assertion**. Mars-ruled rituals involving hemp are bold, intentional, and direct. Using **hemp-based incense** in a Mars ritual amplifies personal power, magnetism, and drive. These rituals are best performed on **Tuesdays** (Mars's day), during **Mars hours** of the planetary clock, and ideally under an Aries moon.

Ritual Example: The Mars Flame Rite

- Create a **triangle of red candles**
- Place a dish of hemp incense (mixed with cinnamon, dragon's blood resin, and black pepper)
- Speak intentions aloud with fire-themed affirmations
- Burn incense as you visualize your obstacles burning away

This rite is ideal for **cutting cords, breaking inertia**, or launching new personal projects with passion.

Aries Moon: Initiating New Hemp-Based Habits

When the moon enters Aries, its lunar rhythm combines with the archetype of initiation. This is an ideal window for **starting new hemp-related habits**, whether it be introducing **hemp nutrition**, **daily smoke rituals**, or using hemp in **fitness or martial arts routines**.

Because Aries moons are fast-moving and electric, this is **not the time for passive reflection**. It's the moment to **act, ignite, and test**.

Try this ritual:

- On the **first night of an Aries moon**, set a hemp intention (e.g., "I commit to sacred hemp tea for 7 days")
- Write it on hemp paper or parchment
- Anoint the paper with infused hemp oil
- Burn it in a safe bowl with a red candle lit beside you

Feel the alignment surge through you. Then begin your new ritual the very next day. Aries supports **bravery through action**.

Combating Burnout with Grounding Hemp Practices

Aries is infamous for its bursts of glory followed by deep crashes. Burnout is common due to the Mars tendency to "go hard or go home." While energizing blends help fuel the fire, grounding hemp practices help **replenish the embers**.

Grounding Practices Include:

- **CBD-rich salves** on the spine and feet
- **Slow-brewed hemp chai** with cardamom and turmeric
- **Body-stretching rituals** combined with hemp-infused balms
- **Root chakra meditations** with hemp-based smudging tools (combine with vetiver, cedar, and patchouli)

These are best done on **earth-sign moon days** (Taurus, Virgo, Capricorn), which help stabilize Aries's hyperdrive. They bring the fire down to the hearth, where it warms rather than consumes.

Conclusion of Chapter 1

For Aries, hemp is more than a plant—it is a **sacred accelerant**, a spiritual matchstick ready to light the soul's path. Through energizing blends, Mars-aligned rituals, and restorative routines, Aries can maintain the delicate balance between **bold pursuit and inner harmony**. Let this chapter serve as your flamekeeper—helping you blaze ahead without burning out.

Chapter 2 – Taurus: The Rooted Flower

Where Aries sparks the flame of beginnings, **Taurus** grounds that fire in earth. Representing **stability, sensuality, and slow, enduring growth**, Taurus is the sacred soil of the zodiac. Ruled by **Venus**, the goddess of beauty, pleasure, and abundance, Taurus invites us to deepen our connection with the body and the material world—through touch, taste, texture, and routine. Hemp, with its nurturing, nourishing, and tactile qualities, is the **perfect plant ally** for this sign.

Taurus doesn't rush. This is a sign that understands **luxury as presence**, not expense. The Taurus path with hemp is about **embodiment, self-worth, and comfort**, making this chapter a sensual sanctuary of ritual, beauty, and abundance.

Earthy Indulgence and Hemp for Sensual Balance

Taurus thrives on groundedness and physical pleasure. Hemp, in this context, becomes a **balancing agent**—soothing anxiety, calming over-stimulation, and heightening the physical senses without overwhelming them. Whether through rich textures, nourishing flavors, or relaxing aromas, the Taurus experience of hemp is deeply **somatic and sensuous**.

To align with Taurus's **earth element**, hemp should be combined with ingredients like:

- **Cacao** – for grounding and opening the heart
- **Cinnamon** – for warmth and inner steadiness
- **Oats** – for comfort and emotional support
- **Rose or vanilla** – for Venusian beauty and softness

The goal is to enter a state of **peaceful embodiment**—a sensory ritual that anchors the spirit into the flesh and reminds you that slowness is sacred.

Earth Element Ritual:

- Lay on a heavy blanket or weighted mat
- Sip warm hemp-infused oat milk with cinnamon
- Light an earthy-scented hemp candle
- Breathe deeply, placing hands over your belly and heart
- Repeat: *"I root, I receive, I rest. My body is sacred ground."*

Venus-Guided Recipes for Hemp-Infused Comfort Foods

As the planetary ruler of Taurus, **Venus** encourages indulgence—not in excess, but in intentional pleasure. Comfort food becomes a **ritual of love**, and hemp elevates it to a healing art. These recipes are ideal during Venus transits, Taurus moons, or anytime you need emotional nourishment or grounding.

Sample Hemp Comfort Recipes:

- **Velvety Hemp Hot Chocolate** (hemp milk + raw cacao + rose syrup + vanilla extract)
- **Hemp Banana Bread with Lavender Honey Glaze**
- **Venusian Hemp Porridge** (hemp hearts + cardamom + figs + cinnamon + crushed pistachio)
- **CBD-Infused Rose & Vanilla Sugar Cookies**
- **Baked Mac and Cheese with Hempseed Crumble Topping**

These foods are best eaten slowly, in a relaxed setting, perhaps during a moon ritual or after a beauty bath. Always add **intention** as the secret ingredient—Taurus energy responds strongly to **emotional presence during creation**.

Hemp Baths, Skincare, and Beauty Rituals

Taurus governs the **physical body and the senses**, especially the **neck, throat, and skin**. Venus amplifies this by calling us to **ritualize self-care as sacred worship**. Hemp is a botanical treasure in skincare and bath rituals due to its anti-inflammatory, moisturizing, and calming properties.

Ritual Bath for Taurus:

- Fill the tub with warm water and add:
    - 1 cup of hemp milk or infused oil
    - ½ cup of Himalayan salt
    - Dried rose petals
    - Few drops of patchouli, ylang-ylang, or vetiver essential oil

Soak while playing soft music, gently massaging the neck and jaw—Taurus tension points. Speak affirmations like: *"I release all pressure. I embrace stillness and softness."*

Beauty & Body Rituals:

- **Face Mask**: hemp seed oil + bentonite clay + rose water
- **Body Scrub**: hemp hearts + brown sugar + vanilla extract + coconut oil
- **Perfume Balm**: beeswax + CBD oil + Venusian oils (rose, jasmine, vanilla)

Perform these rituals especially on **Fridays** (Venus's day) to enhance self-love and magnetism.

Stabilizing Routines with Moon Phases in Taurus

The **Taurus moon** offers fertile soil for creating or strengthening routines. Where other signs crave change or exploration, Taurus seeks predictability and rhythm. Hemp can be integrated into your **daily and lunar-based routines** to stabilize mood, support hormonal cycles, and anchor you to your body.

Sample Taurus Moon Hemp Routine:

- **Morning**: Hemp seed smoothie and grounding affirmations
- **Midday**: CBD salve applied to neck and shoulders during a break
- **Evening**: Hemp tea with lavender and valerian root
- **Night**: Sleep under a weighted blanket with a hemp aromatherapy diffuser

Track your **energy, digestion, and emotions** over several Taurus moon cycles. You'll begin to sense how hemp interacts with your body's seasonal and lunar patterns.

Hemp and Financial Attraction for the Taurus Spirit

Taurus is the **sign of wealth, value, and financial attraction**—not through risk, but through **consistent cultivation**. Hemp, as a crop and sacred plant, embodies this beautifully: it's hearty, regenerative, and yields many forms of abundance. Spiritually, hemp can be used in **rituals for financial stability, prosperity, and material manifestation.**

Financial Ritual: Hemp Prosperity Pouch

- Ingredients:
  - Dried hemp
  - Cinnamon stick
  - Pyrite or green aventurine
  - Bay leaf (write goal amount on it)
  - Small coin

Place all ingredients into a green or gold cloth pouch. Anoint it with **CBD oil and mint essential oil**. Keep in your wallet, desk drawer, or purse.

Moon Timing: Perform under a **waxing Taurus moon** or during a **Venus-in-Taurus transit**. Repeat:
"As this pouch is rooted, so grows my wealth."

Conclusion of Chapter 2

Taurus doesn't just use hemp—it **welcomes it as a guest of honor** in its temple of touch, taste, and tranquility. Through comfort foods, slow rituals, skincare alchemy, and abundance spells, hemp becomes a tool for rooting the spirit deeply into the pleasures of the physical world.

Where Aries ignites, Taurus cultivates. Let this chapter be your **invitation to slow down, indulge mindfully, and grow abundantly**—all with hemp as your sacred garden companion.

Chapter 3 – Gemini: The Dual Leaf

Gemini, the **Messenger of the Zodiac**, dances between polarities—light and shadow, thought and speech, logic and intuition. Represented by the **Twins** and ruled by **Mercury**, Gemini governs **communication, curiosity, intellect, and adaptability**. This is a sign that craves information, thrives on mental stimulation, and often lives with one foot in the material world and the other in the realm of thought.

Hemp, when paired properly with Gemini energy, becomes a **balancer of dualities**, a **mental tuner**, and an **aid for focused communication**. Gemini doesn't want to feel slowed down—it wants to be **clear, expressive, and connected**. This chapter offers a collection of mind-sharpening, breath-focused, and voice-empowering hemp rituals crafted to harmonize with Gemini's quicksilver nature.

Hemp Blends for Mental Clarity and Communication

Gemini thrives on **sharpness of thought**, quick reflexes, and creative problem-solving. However, when overstimulated or overwhelmed, Gemini energy can fragment—scattering attention and fogging focus. Hemp blends for Gemini should support **mental clarity** while grounding nervous energy without dulling curiosity.

Ideal herbs to combine with hemp for Gemini include:

- **Lemon balm** – soothes nerves, enhances cognitive function
- **Gotu kola** – sharpens memory and clarity
- **Peppermint** – awakens mental faculties
- **Blue lotus** – enhances intuitive insight
- **Licorice root** – supports throat chakra and vocal energy

These blends are best used **before writing, speaking, studying, or brainstorming**, either as teas, vaporizable herb mixes, or tinctures.

Mental Clarity Tea Recipe for Gemini:

- 1 tsp hemp flower
- ½ tsp peppermint
- ½ tsp lemon balm
- Dash of licorice root
- Honey (optional)

Sip in a quiet setting with your journal open and mind ready to receive.

Mercury-Ruled Tinctures and Vocal Meditation Aids

As the ruler of Gemini, **Mercury** governs communication, writing, the nervous system, and dexterity. Mercury-aligned tinctures work directly with the **throat chakra**, **lungs**, and **brain pathways**, making them ideal for rituals involving public speaking, teaching, singing, or truth-telling.

A **Mercury-aligned hemp tincture** includes:

- CBD-dominant hemp extract
- Peppermint or eucalyptus oil (to open breath)
- Infusion of citrine or aquamarine (optional crystal elixirs)
- Carried in alcohol or glycerin base
- Activated under a Gemini moon or Mercury hour

Take a dropper under the tongue before **recording a podcast, giving a speech, writing a book, or meditating on your voice**. This is especially potent during **Mercury retrogrades**, when mental fog and communication mishaps are common.

Vocal Meditation Aid:

- Place a drop of tincture on the tongue
- Sit in a calm posture
- Hum softly while placing one hand on your throat and one on your heart
- Inhale deeply and release with sound: "Haaah"
- Repeat: *"My voice is clear. My words are true."*

Herbal Smoke Blends for Expression

Gemini's **air element** makes smoke rituals especially aligned with their essence. Smoke represents ideas made visible—breath made ritual. Hemp smoke blends support **release of tension in the chest and throat**, amplify the connection between mind and breath, and ease anxiety around speaking authentically.

Suggested Smoke Blend for Gemini:

- Hemp flower (balanced or sativa-leaning for mental lift)
- Mugwort (intuition, dream clarity)
- Peppermint (refreshing breath)
- Blue lotus (heart-throat-mind connection)
- A touch of dried orange peel (creativity boost)

Use before **spoken-word rituals**, storytelling circles, or journaling. Blow the smoke in **spirals or figure eights**, symbolic of Gemini's dual yet balanced nature.

Always perform smoke rituals near an open window, honoring the airy nature of Gemini with **breath and movement**.

Scripting Rituals with Hemp Paper Under Gemini Moons

Gemini moons are perfect for **scripting, manifesting through writing, and conscious communication rituals**. During these transits, our minds are faster, ideas more fluid, and insights more likely to flash through from the subconscious.

Using **hemp paper** (sustainable, sacred, and symbolically aligned with the plant's energetic frequency) enhances the ritual. Gemini's Mercury rulership favors writing that is **specific, curious, and mutable**.

Scripting Ritual Steps:

1. Light a candle (yellow or silver)
2. Burn a bit of Gemini smoke blend or hemp incense
3. Sit in front of a blank hemp sheet and write:
    - 3 things you want to learn
    - 3 truths you want to speak
    - 3 conversations you want to initiate
4. Sign your name and draw a Mercury glyph
5. Fold the paper and place it under a speaking crystal (blue lace agate, aquamarine, or clear quartz)

Let this scripting ritual serve as a **contract with your own communication spirit**. You can repeat it each Gemini moon to track growth and clarity.

Adaptability Tools: Hemp for Scattered Focus

While Gemini is brilliant and quick-witted, it is also **prone to distraction, overthinking, and scattered attention**. Hemp offers gentle assistance in **creating focus containers**—rituals, tools, and internal agreements that help Gemini channel their genius into sustained attention.

Focus Rituals with Hemp:

- **CBD balm** rubbed on temples and the back of the neck before deep work
- **Crystal + hemp oil anointing** of your laptop, pen, or voice recorder
- **Hemp-infused focus spray** (distilled water + peppermint + lemon + hemp oil) sprayed in workspaces
- **30-minute ritual focus blocks**: use timer, ritual tea, scent, and music to frame sessions of clarity

Gemini's gift is not in stillness, but in **movement within intention**. Hemp helps create a sacred lens through which Gemini can **choose where to place awareness**, rather than being swept by every passing thought.

Conclusion of Chapter 3

Gemini and hemp together create a **symphony of mind and voice**. Through sharp herbal blends, throat chakra tinctures, sacred scripting, and ritual breathwork, Gemini learns to **communicate with clarity, think with precision, and adapt without losing center**. The dual leaf of hemp honors the dual mind of the Twins—both halves united through sacred breath and sacred green.

May this chapter serve as your **communication compass**, guiding you to think clearly, speak truthfully, and **move with mindful momentum** in your personal world and beyond.

Chapter 4 – Cancer: The Nurturing Leaf

Cancer, the **Moon-ruled guardian of the zodiac**, is the sacred vessel of **emotions, memory, home, and ancestral connection**. Represented by the **Crab**, Cancer's strength lies in its sensitivity, intuition, and ability to hold space for healing. It is the sign of the womb, the tides, the sacred mother, and the spirit of inner sanctuary.

In this watery realm, **hemp becomes a comfort herb, a shield, and a spiritual balm**. Where Gemini seeks stimulation, Cancer seeks safety. Where Aries seeks challenge, Cancer seeks comfort. This chapter explores hemp as a tender companion for emotional release, energetic protection, and ancestral communion.

Emotional Healing and Protection with Hemp

Cancer's deep emotional currents often run beneath the surface. Empathic by nature, this sign can easily absorb other people's energies—sometimes to the point of emotional exhaustion or energetic overwhelm. Hemp, with its calming and grounding nature, becomes a **shield plant** and **emotional restorer** for Cancer individuals.

CBD-rich hemp helps regulate the **nervous system**, soothe anxiety, and reconnect the body with the breath. To Cancer, healing is not linear—it is cyclical, like the moon. Therefore, emotional work with hemp must honor the **ebb and flow of feelings**.

Emotional Healing Techniques for Cancer:

- **Hemp tea + journaling during Full Moons** for emotional release
- **Self-soothing rituals** with CBD oil applied to the chest and shoulders (Cancer's body zones)
- **Weighted blanket + hemp-infused lavender sachet** for comfort and regulation
- **Salt + hemp oil baths** for cleansing absorbed energy

Affirmation:
"I honor my emotions. I restore through softness. I am safe in my inner tide."

Lunar Cycles and Sacred Water + Hemp Infusions
As the only zodiac sign ruled by the **Moon**, Cancer is deeply affected by **lunar cycles**. Each phase of the moon offers Cancer an opportunity to attune, retreat, or expand. When combined with **water rituals and hemp infusions**, these moon phases become **healing ceremonies**.
Moon Phase Rituals:

- **New Moon in Cancer**: Sip a mug of warm hemp-mugwort tea in a candlelit bath. Set intentions for emotional renewal.
- **Waxing Moon**: Create an infusion of **hemp flower + rose + moonstone** in spring water. Let it sit in moonlight and use it as a face splash, room mist, or altar water.
- **Full Moon**: Prepare a **hemp salt bath** with sea salt, crushed hemp leaves, and 3 drops of chamomile essential oil. Light a candle and let go of what no longer nourishes.
- **Waning Moon**: Anoint your solar plexus and heart with **CBD oil + clary sage** while journaling things to release.

Sacred Water Infusion Recipe:

- 2 cups spring water
- 1 tbsp dried hemp leaves or flower
- 1 tsp dried rose petals
- 3 moonstone chips (optional, remove before use)
  Place under the moon for 4–8 hours. Use for spiritual cleansing, ritual rinses, or misting altars.

Ancestral Altar Rituals with Hemp Candles

Cancer holds a deep spiritual connection to **lineage, ancestors, and the home altar**. Creating a **hemp-centered ancestral altar** nourishes the spirit and strengthens the emotional roots of the soul.

How to Create a Hemp Ancestral Altar:

1. Choose a small table or shelf facing east or north.
2. Place a **white or silver cloth** to represent moonlight.
3. Add **photos or symbolic tokens of ancestors** or loved ones.
4. Light **hemp-infused beeswax candles**, anointed with myrrh or mugwort oil.
5. Offer a bowl of **water infused with hemp and sea salt** as a gesture of respect.
6. Speak softly, or write a letter to your ancestors and place it beneath a moonstone.

This altar is most potent when tended to during **Cancer moons** or **Samhain/Day of the Dead**. It serves as a space of **emotional remembrance and protection**.

Comfort Spells: How Cancer Uses Hemp for Security

Comfort is sacred to Cancer. It is not indulgence—it is **emotional necessity**. When the world becomes overwhelming or the spirit feels displaced, Cancer turns to comfort spells to **restore energetic safety** and rebuild inner walls.

Hemp Comfort Spell for Emotional Security:

You'll need:

- A small glass jar
- Dried hemp flower
- A pinch of cinnamon (for warmth)
- Rose quartz chip (for love)
- A lock of hair or handwriting sample (symbol of self)
- Lavender buds

Instructions:

1. Combine ingredients in the jar while saying aloud, *"I build my peace, I claim my calm."*
2. Seal it and anoint with CBD oil.
3. Place it under your bed, near your pillow, or in a coat pocket when leaving home.

Other comfort rituals include:

- **Knit or hand-stitch hemp cloth charms** during new moons
- **Baking hemp-seed cookies with intention** for nurturing self or family
- **Rocking or swaying** while holding a hemp sachet to reset the nervous system

Moonstone and Hemp Charm Bags for Intuition

Cancer's intuition is oceanic. This sign often knows before others know, senses before others speak. But to protect and amplify this gift, Cancer benefits from **charm bags**—small, handmade pouches filled with items that boost psychic sensitivity, emotional protection, and lunar connection.

Intuition Charm Bag Recipe:

- Blue or silver fabric pouch
- 1 tsp dried hemp flower
- 1 moonstone crystal (or amethyst)
- 3 dried jasmine petals (for dream clarity)
- A written affirmation: *"My intuition is sacred and protected."*

Use:

- Tuck under pillow for dreamwork
- Wear during Tarot or divination
- Hold during meditation for intuitive strengthening
- Place on third eye during moon rituals

Cancer intuitively connects to the **astral and dream realms**, making this charm ideal for nighttime visions, ancestral contact, or psychic journaling.

Conclusion of Chapter 4

Cancer and hemp share a bond of **nurturing essence and healing rhythm**. Together, they teach the sacred art of **emotional safety, lunar intuition, and ancestral love**. Hemp becomes a gentle tide that rocks the inner child, an herbal balm for the wounded heart, and a root that grounds the spirit in a world of shifting sands.

Let this chapter be your **emotional sanctuary**. With every hemp infusion, ancestral prayer, moon ritual, and charm crafted with care, may you rediscover the **security within your softness** and the **strength hidden in your sensitivity**.

Chapter 5 – Leo: The Radiant Bud

Leo, the **lion-hearted performer of the zodiac**, radiates confidence, charisma, and creative fire. Ruled by the **Sun**, Leo represents the **center of identity, expression, and self-worth**. It is the sign of performers, leaders, lovers, and creators—those who shine not for validation, but because their inner light simply cannot be hidden.

In this regal context, **hemp becomes a source of solar amplification**—a botanical ally that magnifies inner brilliance, nourishes confidence, and fuels passion with grounded poise. Where Cancer retreats inward, Leo emerges boldly, sharing its gifts with the world. And yet, Leo's flame also needs tending—a balance of pride and humility, power and peace.

This chapter explores how hemp can be used to **enhance Leo's fire without burnout**, amplify magnetism, and serve as a **ritual companion** for artistic expression, leadership, and romantic devotion.

Hemp Rituals for Creativity, Confidence, and Performance

Creativity is the life-force of Leo. Whether it's art, movement, speech, or simply how they show up in the world, Leos are born to express. But self-doubt and fear of being unseen can block the natural flow of their creative spirit. Hemp rituals offer support by softening performance anxiety, increasing self-trust, and grounding the ego into authentic self-expression.

Confidence Ritual Before Performance:

1. Inhale a hemp-based herbal blend containing **lemongrass, rosemary, and hemp flower** (ideal as vapor or smoke).
2. Apply **CBD-infused body oil** over the heart and throat chakras.
3. Stand in front of a mirror and say:
   "I am seen. I am sovereign. I shine with divine brilliance."
4. Perform a short expressive movement—dance, vocal warm-up, or power pose.
5. Visualize golden light entering your crown and radiating outward.

This ritual can be done before any high-pressure situation: public speaking, interviews, auditions, or important conversations.

Sun-Aligned Energizing Hemp Practices

As the only zodiac sign ruled by the **Sun**, Leo finds power in **daylight-based rituals**, **solar timing**, and **radiant movement**. Hemp used in the morning or early afternoon can amplify solar alignment, especially in the form of **energizing teas, oils, and sun-charged salves**.

Morning Solar Hemp Practice:

- Drink a **sun tea** brewed the day before, made of:
    - Hemp flower
    - Dried orange peel
    - Calendula (for solar clarity)
    - Cinnamon stick (for fire and vitality)

Let the tea sit in the sun for at least 4 hours in a clear glass jar. Consume while facing the sunrise or standing barefoot on the earth. Visualize the sun's light charging your solar plexus.

Additionally, use **CBD body balms or rollers** mid-day to refresh energy, especially on your chest and shoulders—Leo's ruling body areas.

Rituals for Leadership and Attention Using Solar-Charged Hemp Oil

Leo doesn't just perform—it **leads**. Solar hemp oil rituals awaken the inner leader and build confidence in being witnessed. These rituals should be **simple, potent, and visible**, embodying Leo's natural magnetism.

How to Solar-Charge Hemp Oil:

1. Fill a glass bottle with **CBD oil** (or hemp seed oil).
2. Add dried **chamomile, marigold, and orange peel**.
3. Place it in direct sunlight for 3–5 hours during a **Sun in Leo** transit, or on a **Sunday** (Sun's day).
4. Shake gently and set the intention: *"With this oil, I lead with grace, strength, and light."*

Solar Leadership Ritual:

- Rub solar oil on your temples and heart
- Light a **gold or orange candle**
- Write down your leadership intention ("I lead a team," "I launch my vision," etc.)
- Read it aloud, then burn it as an offering to the Sun
- Speak the Leo invocation: *"As the Sun never asks for praise, I too rise by nature's right."*

Repeat this on the **New Moon or Full Moon in Leo**, or before any leadership endeavor.

Hemp Self-Love Mirrors and Leo Affirmations

Leo's greatest challenge is self-worth without external applause. True Leo power comes from **radiating without needing reflection**—yet using mirrors in a **sacred way** can reinforce healthy ego and deep inner validation.

Mirror Ritual with Hemp:

1. Set up a **mirror altar** with a gold cloth, a candle, a bottle of CBD oil, and citrine or tiger's eye.
2. Apply a **drop of hemp oil to your forehead and heart**.
3. Light the candle and gaze into your eyes in the mirror.
4. Speak aloud:
   - *"I am my own light."*
   - *"I deserve to shine."*
   - *"My joy is medicine to the world."*

This can be performed weekly for **confidence maintenance**, especially during periods of doubt or invisibility.

Leo-Specific Affirmations:

- "I honor the royalty of my spirit."
- "My brilliance inspires, not intimidates."
- "I allow myself to be adored without shrinking."
- "Creativity flows through me like sunlight."

Writing these on hemp paper and placing them on a vision board or altar boosts the power.

Fiery Passion Blends for Leo's Romantic Flair

Ruled by the **Sun** and the **Heart**, Leo is a **lover**—romantic, loyal, and passionate. Hemp used in sensual and romantic rituals can open Leo's heart, heighten physical touch, and increase emotional intimacy.

Sensual Hemp Blend:

- Hemp flower (relaxation + heart energy)
- Damiana (aphrodisiac + mood booster)
- Rose petals (love and Venus)
- Cinnamon (passion and magnetism)
- Orange blossom or vanilla (warmth and sweetness)

Smoke, steep, or burn as incense before romantic encounters. Alternatively, craft a **romantic oil blend** for massage or bath:

- Hemp oil + damiana tincture + rose essential oil + vanilla extract
- Charge under a Full Moon in Leo

Use this oil during a **shared bath ritual**, couples massage, or solo self-love ceremony.

Passion Ritual:

- Place red and gold candles in a circle
- In the center, write your desires for love and intimacy on hemp parchment
- Burn the note while anointing yourself with sensual hemp oil
- Speak aloud: *"I attract what ignites and nourishes."*

Conclusion of Chapter 5

Leo teaches us that **shining is not arrogance—it's alignment**. With the right rituals, hemp becomes Leo's sacred herb of brilliance: a botanical amplifier of joy, expression, leadership, and sensual fire. It supports the lion's roar and the gentle purr, the bold speech and the private dance of self-adoration.

Let this chapter be your **stage and sanctuary**. With every tea, ritual, and affirmation, you claim the power of radiant presence—not because others demand it, but because your soul was born to shine.

Chapter 6 – Virgo: The Purified Plant

Virgo, the **Earth Priestess of the Zodiac**, represents **purity, service, order, and refinement**. Symbolized by the Virgin—not in the sense of abstinence, but of sacred sovereignty—Virgo holds the power of the **healer, the herbalist, and the alchemist**. Governed by **Mercury**, Virgo connects the intellect with embodiment, turning thought into organized practice and chaos into clarity.

For Virgo, hemp becomes not just a tool, but a ritual assistant—a plant that helps clear the fog, soothe the gut, regulate the nervous system, and create harmony in both body and space. This chapter explores how Virgo uses hemp to **cleanse, realign, and regenerate**, crafting practical magic from mindful routine.

Cleanse, Detox, and Organize with Hemp

Virgo's domain is **health and routine**, and its innate desire is to bring **cleanliness and balance** to all systems—whether in the body, the home, or the schedule. Hemp can support Virgo's mission by functioning as a **cleansing agent** for the body and an **energetic purifier** for the environment.

Internal Cleansing:

- Hemp's high fiber content (especially hemp seeds) aids **colon health and toxin elimination**.
- **CBD tinctures** help reduce inflammation, support gut lining repair, and regulate cortisol (the stress hormone).
- Virgo thrives with **ritual detoxing**, especially during waning moons or seasonal shifts.

Daily Virgo Detox Ritual:

- Morning: Warm lemon water + 1 tsp hemp seed oil
- Midday: Light meal with hemp seeds, greens, and ginger
- Evening: Herbal detox tea with hemp flower, fennel, and dandelion root

External Organizing:

- Declutter and realign your **workspace**, **bedroom**, or **altar** while diffusing **hemp essential oil + rosemary**
- Clean surfaces using a natural hemp-oil based spray with lemon, mint, and white vinegar
- Assign symbolic meanings to areas of your home (e.g., bathroom = purification; kitchen = nourishment) and organize with intention

Affirmation:

"I cleanse to make space. I align to remember who I am."

Mercury-Ruled Teas for Digestion and Clarity

As Virgo's ruling planet, **Mercury** governs the **nervous system and the intestines**—two realms deeply interconnected. Many Virgos experience digestive issues related to anxiety, overthinking, or perfectionism. Enter hemp: a grounding herb that nurtures both clarity and calm digestion.

Digestive Clarity Tea for Virgo:

- 1 tsp dried hemp flower (CBD-rich)
- ½ tsp fennel seeds (for bloating)
- ½ tsp lemon balm (soothes nerves)
- Pinch of dried ginger (boosts digestion)
- Optional: raw honey (gut-friendly prebiotic)

Sip this slowly after meals or while journaling. It clears both **mental clutter** and **physical tension** in the gut. Best used during Mercury transits or stressful days when your **gut-brain axis** feels dysregulated.

Using Hemp for Scheduling and Sleep Improvement

Virgo rules the **sixth house of health, habits, and daily structure**. It is the master of planners, lists, and intentional routine. But with that comes **mental fatigue, sleep struggles, and obsessive thinking**—especially at night. Hemp provides gentle support for **routine reinforcement and circadian reset**.

Hemp for Scheduling:

- Begin your week with a **ritual planning session** using:
    - A calming tea made of hemp, peppermint, and tulsi
    - A candle infused with rosemary and hemp scent
    - A journal or planner crafted with hemp paper

Write out your week's intentions with clarity. Use color-coded highlighters, break your days into manageable blocks, and include **rest as a non-negotiable task**.

Hemp for Sleep:

- 1 hour before bed: Take a **CBD tincture** or capsule
- Use a **hemp + lavender sleep spray** on your pillow
- Perform a **Virgo grounding stretch** (child's pose, forward fold, gentle twists)
- Play binaural beats or delta-wave music while holding a **moonstone or amethyst + hemp sachet**

Virgo Sleep Affirmation:
"I release today's order. I trust tomorrow's unfolding."

Creating a Sacred Hemp-Smudge Cleaning Ritual

Virgo's energetic sensitivity often draws it to sacred cleanliness—not just sterile tidiness, but **energetic hygiene**. Virgo can transform house-cleaning into a powerful **magickal ritual** using hemp as a purifying herb.

Sacred Hemp-Smudge Ritual:

1. Blend **dried hemp leaves**, **rosemary**, and **sage** into a smudge bundle or loose-leaf bowl.
2. Open windows to allow stagnant energy to leave.
3. As you move through the home, speak aloud:
   "With hemp and herb, I cleanse this space. May peace return and chaos erase."
4. Pay special attention to doorways, corners, and beds.
5. After smudging, diffuse **hemp oil + lemon balm** and light a **white candle**.

Do this weekly or on **Virgo moon days**, especially after guests leave or intense emotional days.

Virgo New Moon Hemp Reset Ceremonies

The **New Moon in Virgo** is one of the most powerful times for **health resets, habit building, and intentional living**. Virgo loves structure, so crafting a **step-by-step moon ritual with hemp** speaks directly to its spiritual instincts.

Hemp Reset Ceremony (New Moon in Virgo):
Supplies:

- A clean journal
- Hemp-infused bath or foot soak
- Green candle (for healing and growth)
- Ritual tea (hemp, nettle, lemon balm)

Steps:

1. **Cleanse your body** with a hemp bath or soak. Visualize impurities dissolving.
2. Light the green candle and sip your tea.
3. Write 3 health goals and 3 organizational goals on hemp paper. Be specific.
4. For each goal, draw a tiny leaf or root beside it (to symbolize growth).
5. Fold the list and place it under a **piece of moss agate, jade, or clear quartz** on your altar.
6. Speak aloud:

   "I plant these goals with care and devotion. I grow in alignment with my truth."

Repeat this ceremony each year, or adapt it monthly to track subtle progress. Virgo thrives in the **refinement of intention** over time.

Conclusion of Chapter 6

Virgo and hemp are sacred allies in the **art of sacred structure, grounded healing, and inner order**. Through cleansing rituals, digestion-focused teas, restful routines, and smudging ceremonies, Virgo finds peace not in perfection—but in **purposeful process**.

Let this chapter serve as your **ritual guide to mindful order**. May you remember that the divine lives in detail, that wellness is a daily devotion, and that hemp is your trusted plant companion in the graceful, earthy journey toward wholeness.

Chapter 7 – Libra: The Harmonizing Leaf

Libra, the **sign of balance, beauty, and sacred relationship**, is ruled by **Venus**—the planet of love, aesthetics, and interpersonal harmony. Symbolized by the **Scales**, Libra represents the search for **equilibrium between self and other**, desire and duty, thought and feeling. It is the zodiac's natural peacemaker, artist, diplomat, and mirror.

When combined with Libra's graceful energy, **hemp becomes a sacred balancer**—a plant of elegance, neutrality, and energetic cohesion. It softens conflict, refines perception, and supports both inner and outer alignment. Whether working through indecision, strengthening a partnership, or restoring energetic equilibrium, hemp acts as Libra's **botanical peacekeeper and beauty ally**.

This chapter explores how Libra can use hemp to cultivate harmony in relationships, ritual beauty, spiritual fairness, and energetic symmetry.

Hemp for Balance, Relationships, and Decision-Making

Libra's mind is wired for **weighing both sides**, but this gift can often result in **paralysis by analysis**. Hemp's calming and centering properties help **quiet mental overprocessing**, reduce anxiety around choices, and ground Libra in the heart rather than endless hypotheticals.

Decision-Making Ritual:

1. Brew a tea of **hemp flower**, **lemon verbena**, and **white tea**.
2. Sit with two candles—one white, one blue—representing both choices or paths.
3. Place a **rose quartz** in front of you.
4. Sip tea slowly, then journal with the prompt:
   "Which path brings greater peace, not just possibility?"
5. Place your hand over your heart and speak:
   "I choose balance over pressure. I choose alignment over fear."

For relationship decisions, repeat the ritual under a **Libra Moon**, using **paired crystals** (like twin moonstones) and hemp smoke to help calm the heart and mind.

Venus-Blessed Oils and Beauty Treatments

Libra, as a **Venus-ruled sign**, flourishes in self-care rituals that are not only nurturing but *aesthetic* and *refining*. Hemp, known for its **skin-soothing and anti-inflammatory** properties, becomes a luxurious base for Libra's beauty and charm-enhancing practices.

Venus-Infused Hemp Face Oil:

- 2 oz **cold-pressed hemp seed oil**
- 5 drops **rose essential oil**
- 2 drops **geranium** (for hormonal balance)
- 3 drops **ylang-ylang** (for sensual magnetism)
- Optional: a small piece of rose quartz placed inside the bottle for energy infusion

Massage into clean skin during the **Venus hour** on **Fridays**. Whisper affirmations such as:
"My glow is divine. My beauty is harmony made visible."

Additional Venusian Hemp Treatments:

- **Hemp & clay facial masks** for clarity and smoothness
- **Hemp rose lip balm** for soft, kissable lips
- **Hair oiling with hemp + jasmine** for shine and energetic softness
- **CBD massage oil** for tension release in the shoulders and lower back (Libra's ruled zones)

Pairing Hemp and Rose in Bath Spells

Rose is **Venus's sacred flower**, representing love, softness, and the open heart. When paired with hemp in **ritual baths**, the result is **emotional repair, energetic beautification, and relationship rebalancing**.

Libra Love & Harmony Bath:

- 1 cup **hemp milk** or **CBD-infused bath oil**
- 1 handful of **rose petals (pink or red)**
- 1 tsp of **Himalayan salt** (for aura cleansing)
- 3 drops **rose or vanilla oil**
- Optional: small floating candles in pink or white

Set intentions before entering the bath:
"I call in harmony. I soak in beauty. I restore my center."

Play soft music, hold a rose quartz in your left hand, and visualize tension dissolving into the water. Let this bath be an **act of self-love and energetic symmetry**, especially after emotionally intense social interactions or conflicts.

Hemp Justice Spells and Equilibrium Talismans

Libra is the zodiac's **archetype of justice and fairness**—not punishment, but **restorative balance**. Hemp can be incorporated into **rituals for ethical clarity, boundary healing, and karmic neutrality**.

Justice Spell with Hemp and Feather:

Materials:

- Dried **hemp flower or leaf**
- A **white feather** (symbol of Maat, the goddess of truth)
- A small **scales charm** or drawn image
- A candle in **sky blue** (for truth and diplomacy)
- Parchment or hemp paper

Steps:

1. Write the injustice or imbalance you wish to resolve.
2. Fold the paper and wrap it in the feather with hemp twine.
3. Place on your altar beside the candle and scales symbol.
4. Say aloud:

   "By air and earth, may truth arise. By balance born, let wrongs revise."
5. Burn the paper safely, or bury it in your garden or plant pot.

Equilibrium Talisman:

Combine in a pouch:

- Hemp leaves
- Lavender (for calm)
- Black tourmaline (for grounding)
- Lapis lazuli (for truth)
- A written phrase: *"I walk the line between heart and mind."*

Carry it during court proceedings, difficult conversations, or decision-making days.

Partner Rituals Using Hemp to Unite Energies

Libra thrives in **partnerships**—romantic, creative, or spiritual. These connections nourish the Libra soul, and hemp can help deepen that bond through **rituals that honor shared growth, clarity, and intimacy**.

Hemp Unity Candle Ritual:

Materials:

- One **hemp-wrapped candle** or a **dual-wick candle**
- 2 cups of **hemp rose tea** (one for each partner)
- Two stones (rose quartz, moonstone, or emerald)
- Shared written intention: "We co-create balance and love."

Steps:

1. Sit facing one another. Light the candle together.
2. Drink your tea slowly, alternating sips.
3. Speak one word each back and forth that represents what you bring to the relationship.
4. Close by placing the two stones on either side of the candle and saying:
   "As hemp grounds and rose softens, may our bond be both rooted and blossoming."

This ritual can be done monthly or during **Full Moons in Libra**, **anniversaries**, or **creative partnerships** launching a new phase.

Conclusion of Chapter 7

Libra and hemp create a sacred alliance for **grace, beauty, balance, and connection**. Whether used to calm decision anxiety, soothe the skin, enchant a relationship, or restore cosmic fairness, hemp becomes Libra's botanical mirror—offering peace where there is tension, softness where there is friction, and radiant love where there is doubt.

Let this chapter be your guide to **harmonizing all your relationships**—with others, the cosmos, and most importantly, yourself. When the world wavers, return to the center. Hemp and Libra together will lead you back to balance.

Chapter 8 – Scorpio: The Shadow Root

Scorpio, the **alchemist of the zodiac,** is a sign of **depth, transformation, secrecy, power, and resurrection**. Ruled by **Pluto**—planet of death, rebirth, and the subconscious—Scorpio moves beneath the surface, through shadows, emotions, and buried truths. Where other signs seek light, Scorpio **honors the dark**, knowing that healing requires diving into the unseen.

Hemp, in Scorpio's world, becomes a **ritual herb of metamorphosis**. It soothes pain while unlocking secrets. It grounds the body while unraveling psychic knots. It becomes a sacred tool for **sexual empowerment, shadow integration, emotional intensity, and mystical power**.

This chapter invites you into Scorpio's **inner sanctum**, showing how hemp can be used in **deep rituals of transformation, psychic awakening, and release**. This is the path of the **Shadow Root**—the plant's essence not only as life-giver, but as gatekeeper of the underworld.

Hemp for Transformation, Secrets, and Sexual Alchemy

Scorpio governs the **sacral chakra**, sexuality, and psychic boundaries. Its magic is not soft—it is primal, erotic, transformative. Hemp in this realm becomes more than calming—it becomes **initiatory**. Used with intention, it can unlock sacred sexual energy, draw out repressed truths, and guide emotional transmutation.

Hemp and Sexual Alchemy:

- Use **CBD-infused massage oils** during tantric practices or solo pleasure for unlocking **sacral energy**
- Add **hemp + damiana + cacao** to an aphrodisiac tea to awaken sensual awareness and vulnerability
- Create a **sensual altar** with black candles, hemp smoke, and rose quartz for magnetism and trust
- Practice **mirror touch rituals** with hemp anointing, affirming your body's sacred intelligence

Scorpio seeks **depth, not distraction**—so any sexual ritual must be **intentional, honest, and emotionally charged**.

Sexual Alchemy Affirmation:
"I release shame. I embrace power. My body is both portal and priestess."

Pluto-Aligned Hemp Underworld Meditations

Pluto's energy is subtle, intense, and often invisible. It rules **initiation, the soul's death cycles, and hidden truths**. Working with Pluto and hemp allows Scorpio to enter the **inner underworld**—not to escape, but to **transform from within**.

Underworld Meditation Ritual:

1. Prepare a **darkened ritual space** with black cloth, a bowl of water, and a **CBD tincture**.
2. Take a small dose and allow it to settle. Sit with **deep rhythmic breath**.
3. Light a **black or deep indigo candle**. Speak:
   "I descend to remember. I return with power."
4. Visualize a spiral staircase beneath your feet, leading to an **underworld temple**.
5. Meet an archetype (a guide, animal, ancestor, or version of yourself). Ask:
   "What must I let go of to reclaim my truth?"
6. Journal your answers after your return.

Use this meditation during **Pluto transits, Scorpio Moons, or eclipses**, when psychic veils thin and rebirth becomes inevitable.

Shadow Work with Hemp Candles and Ritual Smokes

Scorpio governs **shadow work**—the conscious exploration of the unconscious. It means facing parts of ourselves we fear, deny, or repress. Hemp assists by **lowering resistance**, softening defenses, and opening emotional portals.

Shadow Work Setup:

- Light a **black hemp-infused candle** (blend with myrrh, patchouli, or vetiver oils)
- Use a **ritual smoke blend** of:
  - Hemp flower (truth and opening)
  - Mugwort (vision and dreams)
  - Clove (purification)
  - Dried blood orange peel (emotional courage)

As smoke rises, write:

- 3 behaviors or patterns you fear to admit
- 3 emotions you avoid feeling
- 3 truths you've buried beneath identity

Burn the paper safely, then sit in stillness. Scorpio transformation doesn't happen through avoidance—it comes through **ritual presence in the dark**.

Shadow Affirmation:

"I am whole, including what I hide. I am power, not despite my wounds, but because of them."

Binding and Release Ceremonies During Scorpio Moons

Scorpio moons, especially **New and Full Moons,** carry immense emotional intensity and magic. These are ideal times for **binding toxic patterns, releasing outdated ties, and reclaiming sovereignty**.

Scorpio Moon Binding & Release Ritual:

You'll need:

- Black string or cord
- Hemp leaf or bud
- Small slip of paper
- Fireproof dish or cauldron
- Candle (red for release, black for protection)

Steps:

1. Write the name, habit, or emotion you're releasing.
2. Wrap the hemp leaf and paper together with the black cord.
3. Hold over the flame and say:
   "With truth as fire, I release what binds. I sever what no longer serves."
4. Burn or bury the bundle.

Do this on a **Full Moon in Scorpio** to release attachments. On a **New Moon,** write what new self you're calling in and bury a hemp seed alongside the intention to symbolize rebirth.

Hemp + Obsidian Charm Crafting

Scorpio protects what is sacred. **Psychic shielding** is vital for this sign, and creating **talismans from hemp and obsidian** offers both spiritual armor and emotional protection.

Obsidian + Hemp Protection Charm:
Ingredients:

- Small black pouch
- Crushed dried hemp
- One piece of **black obsidian**
- Sprig of rosemary
- Small sigil or glyph drawn for protection

Steps:

1. Infuse the pouch with **intentional breath**: inhale deeply, hold the pouch at your chest, exhale slowly.
2. Visualize a black mist forming a **shield around your aura**.
3. Say:
   "I walk unseen to harm. I see, but am not seen by shadow."

Carry this charm during vulnerable moments, in spiritual work, or after emotionally draining interactions.

You may also create **hemp-bound obsidian bracelets or anklets** with cord to wear during ritual or dreamwork.

Conclusion of Chapter 8

Scorpio and hemp share a sacred role: **guides through the underworld, keepers of transformation, and guardians of power**. Whether through sexual alchemy, ancestral healing, shadow work, or psychic protection, hemp empowers Scorpio to move **deeper into truth and higher into strength**.

Let this chapter serve as your **initiation into self-sovereignty**. Here, your pain becomes your power, your secrets become your spells, and your fear becomes your freedom. The Shadow Root is not your weakness—it's your source.

Chapter 9 – Sagittarius: The Explorer's Herb

Sagittarius, the **eternal wanderer of the zodiac**, is ruled by **Jupiter**, planet of **expansion, higher learning, philosophy, and adventure**. This fire sign is driven by a sacred hunger—not only to travel the world but to explore the truth of existence, question boundaries, and transcend limitations. Sagittarius thrives when it is free, inspired, and oriented toward purpose beyond the material.

In this bold context, **hemp becomes the herbal compass**—a plant of exploration, elevation, and philosophical integration. Where Virgo organizes, and Scorpio transforms, Sagittarius *soars*—and hemp acts as both tether and launchpad. It anchors the body while expanding the mind, facilitates lucid insight while maintaining warmth and humor, and transforms rituals into journeys of cosmic proportion.

This chapter explores how Sagittarius can use hemp for **soulful adventure, visionary dreaming, spiritual journaling, and sacred fire offerings**—fueled always by the restless heartbeat of the cosmic traveler.

Hemp Blends for Adventure, Truth-Seeking, and Learning

Sagittarius is associated with the **thighs, hips, and liver**—the parts of the body that move us forward and process freedom and detoxification. But Sag's wild spirit can lead to **burnout, overstimulation, or scattered focus** if not tempered.

Hemp, combined with herbs that enhance **exploration, travel endurance, and philosophical clarity**, becomes the perfect companion for long trips, study binges, or spontaneous quests.

Truth-Seeker's Herbal Hemp Blend:

- **Hemp flower** (CBD-rich or balanced) – grounding and expansive
- **Holy basil (tulsi)** – for adaptability and mental clarity
- **Sage** – for protection on the journey
- **Lemongrass or orange peel** – for optimism and lift
- **Ginger root** – to stoke fire and support digestion on the road

Use this blend in:

- **Teas** before or during travel
- **Smoke rituals** before philosophical inquiry
- **Infusions** during late-night study sessions or goal-mapping

Sagittarius Mantra:

"My curiosity is sacred. My journey is eternal. I follow where truth calls me."

Jupiter-Enhanced Travel Rituals with Hemp Talismans

Ruled by **Jupiter**, the great cosmic benefactor, Sagittarius aligns best with **abundance spells, travel charms, and expansive blessings**. When traveling—physically or spiritually—hemp can be fashioned into protective talismans that magnetize luck, spiritual growth, and safe passage.

Jupiter Travel Ritual:

1. Create a **small pouch** filled with:
   - Dried **hemp**
   - A **Jupiter-ruled stone** (amethyst, turquoise, or lapis lazuli)
   - A pinch of **clove** and **bay leaf** (for safe journeys)
   - A map or written name of your destination
2. Anoint the pouch with **hemp oil + citrus oil** (grapefruit or orange).
3. Light a **blue candle** (Jupiter's color) and say:
   "By sky, root, and flame, I travel with truth. Jupiter, bless my path."
4. Carry the talisman in your bag, glovebox, or pocket.

Repeat before each journey—especially international trips or life-changing relocations. This also supports **spiritual pilgrimages or retreats**.

Expanding Consciousness Through Hemp Dreaming

Sagittarius loves to expand the mind. While psychedelics or plant medicine are often associated with this sign, **dreamwork is its quieter counterpart**—a realm of symbolic learning, astral travel, and mythic guidance. Hemp assists by **relaxing the nervous system**, reducing sleep disturbances, and opening the intuitive field for **lucid dreaming and philosophical insight**.

Dream Expansion Ritual:

- 1 hour before bed, take a tea of:
  - **Hemp flower**
  - **Mugwort** (lucid dreaming and astral clarity)
  - **Blue lotus** (spiritual dreaming)
  - **Chamomile** (emotional integration)
- Place a **journal, pen, and a piece of sodalite or lapis** beside your bed.
- Anoint your third eye with **CBD oil + lavender**.
- Speak:
  "I open the temple of my mind. I receive what the stars whisper."

Use this ritual during **Jupiter transits, Sagittarius moons**, or when seeking dream-based answers.

Hemp Journaling for Philosophical Downloads

Sagittarius is the **scribe of spiritual fire**—writing not just for self-reflection but to make sense of the universe. Journaling with hemp becomes a **ritual of truth-extraction**, where insights emerge between the lines, and cosmic teachings download through ink.

Philosophical Journaling Practice:

1. Brew **hemp + rosemary + lemon balm** tea for mental clarity
2. Sit near a window or under sunlight
3. Set a timer for 33 minutes (Jupiter's numerological alignment)
4. Use prompts such as:
    ◦ "What truth is trying to find me?"
    ◦ "Where have I grown beyond my beliefs?"
    ◦ "What does freedom mean to me today?"
5. Let yourself write without censorship—this is a **channeling session**, not analysis

For deeper integration, burn a small **hemp-infused candle** while writing. When finished, read what you wrote aloud as a declaration of evolving truth.

Fire Rituals with Hemp Offerings

Sagittarius is a **mutable fire sign**, ever-shifting and rekindling. **Fire rituals** are essential to the Sagittarian soul. Hemp offerings can be used in sacred flames to **release limitations, energize intentions, and invoke cosmic wisdom**.

Hemp Fire Offering Ceremony:
Supplies:

- Small fire pit or heat-safe bowl
- Dried **hemp leaves or hemp parchment**
- Your written limiting belief, burned into a symbol or statement
- Cinnamon or clove (to feed the flame)
- Optional: map or photo of a destination

Steps:

1. On a **Sagittarius New or Full Moon**, light your fire safely.
2. Place your offering (written belief, doubt, or resistance) on hemp paper into the flame.
3. Add dried hemp and say:
   "As hemp burns, so too my bindings. As fire grows, so too my wisdom."
4. Dance, drum, or move around the fire. Call out your next destination—physical, emotional, or spiritual.
5. Close with deep breath and quiet gratitude.

This ritual renews your purpose, awakens your path, and honors the **wild fire of Sagittarius**—a fire that wanders, but never fades.

Conclusion of Chapter 9

Sagittarius and hemp walk hand-in-hand through **unmapped lands of insight and inspiration**. Together, they birth sacred fire, wisdom quests, and expanding skies. With every tea blend, travel charm, dream journey, and fire ritual, the Sagittarius soul burns away limitations and steps into **a truth too big to hold—but sacred enough to chase forever**.

Let this chapter be your **passport to higher ground**. In your search for meaning, hemp is not the destination—it is the steady flame that walks beside you, whispering: *"Go further. Ask more. Become the question."*

Chapter 10 – Capricorn: The Sacred Structure

Capricorn, the **builder and architect of the zodiac**, is ruled by **Saturn**, the planet of **discipline, time, legacy, and material mastery**. Represented by the **Sea-Goat**, Capricorn combines **earth-bound resilience** with a quiet spiritual depth, climbing mountains on the physical plane while carrying ancient wisdom in its depths.

Where Sagittarius soars with vision, Capricorn **builds the steps to reach it**. In this context, **hemp becomes a stabilizing, focus-enhancing ally**—a plant that encourages long-term thinking, helps manage stress from leadership or responsibility, and assists in creating spiritual infrastructure for success.

This chapter explores how Capricorn can use hemp for **grounded manifestation, career-aligned ritual, financial elevation, and sacred altar design**. This is where hemp is not just a plant—it is a **pillar in the temple of your legacy**.

Hemp for Discipline, Focus, and Manifestation

Capricorn thrives when purpose is clarified and systems are in place to execute it. Yet, this sign often carries the weight of expectations—both external and self-imposed. Hemp becomes Capricorn's **mental compass and nervous system stabilizer**, allowing focus and discipline to flourish without rigidity or burnout.

Hemp Focus Ritual (Morning Practice):

- Brew a cup of **hemp + rosemary + lion's mane mushroom** tea
- Light a single **white or gray candle**
- Sit with your planner or journal
- Write down 3 tasks you commit to today
- Apply **CBD oil** behind the ears and say:
  "I honor the mountain. I take the next step with power."

This ritual, repeated daily, brings **clarity, calm, and committed execution**. Hemp eases mental overactivity while sharpening resolve.

Saturn-Blessed Financial Ritual Blends

Saturn governs **karma, structure, and earned wealth**. It rewards consistency, maturity, and delayed gratification. Capricorn rules the **10th house**—career, reputation, and public success. Hemp used in **Saturn-aligned rituals** becomes a tool of **financial grounding and long-term wealth attraction**.

Saturn Ritual Blend:

- **Hemp flower** (CBD-dominant for focus)
- **Patchouli** (earthy abundance)
- **Vetiver root** (deep anchoring)
- **Frankincense** (spiritual legacy)
- **Crushed black pepper** (Saturn spice for clarity and courage)

Use this blend as:

- A **smoke ritual** before making important business decisions
- A **tea** before reviewing finances or planning income streams
- A **bowl of loose herbs** charged on your altar with obsidian and a coin

Speak:
"By root and rule, I build my rise. By Saturn's clock, I craft my climb."

Success-Focused Tinctures and Grounding Smokes

In Capricorn rituals, success isn't rushed—it's engineered. Hemp-based tinctures can help regulate **nervous system tension**, support mental endurance, and build a sustainable work rhythm. Meanwhile, grounding smoke blends recalibrate the body during intense work periods or after professional exhaustion.

Capricorn Tincture Recipe (Success Support):

- Base: **CBD oil or glycerin extract**
- Add:
    - **Ashwagandha tincture** (adaptogen for stress)
    - **Ginger root** (warmth and motivation)
    - **Black walnut hull** (resilience and protection)
    - Optional: **clear quartz chip** (clarity)

Take this tincture before **goal-setting, business meetings, or creative planning**.

Grounding Smoke Blend (End of Day):

- **Hemp flower**
- **Lavender buds**
- **Cedar shavings**
- **Dried basil**
- Burn in a heat-safe bowl. Sit in silence and allow the day's pressure to lift away.

Capricorn Mantra:
"I do not rush. I do not fall. I rise with rooted will."

Goal Manifestation Spells with Structured Lunar Cycles

Capricorn's earth element works best with **visible progress and defined steps**. When paired with lunar cycles, Capricorn can **harness time as a sacred technology**—using **waxing moons to build, full moons to affirm, and waning moons to revise**.

Capricorn Lunar Manifestation Framework:

- **New Moon**: Define ONE main goal. Write it on hemp paper. Bury a hemp seed in soil with the intention.
- **Waxing Moon**: Take action. Schedule tasks weekly. Use hemp tea + frankincense incense to fuel the vision.
- **Full Moon**: Review progress. Place your goal under moonlight with a quartz + pyrite crystal grid.
- **Waning Moon**: Reflect and refine. Burn or compost the original note. Write a new version that reflects current clarity.

Tools:

- Planner or digital tracker
- Hemp-infused ritual ink for writing
- Crystals: Pyrite, Black Onyx, Obsidian
- A calendar aligned with moon phases

Capricorn doesn't manifest by wishing—it **manifests by working smart within cosmic rhythm**.

Altar Building with Hemp and Obsidian
Capricorn altars are **minimal, powerful, and timeless**. They're not for show—they're for **grounding energy, commanding focus, and honoring lineage**. Hemp and obsidian form a sacred alliance here: **hemp as the earth's breath, obsidian as its ancestral core**.
Building a Capricorn-Aligned Altar:

1. Use a **wooden or stone base**, cleaned with hemp oil + rosemary
2. Place items with clear intention and symmetry:
    ◦ **Obsidian**: Protection, ancestral connection
    ◦ **Hemp rope or woven cloth**: Symbol of endurance and resilience
    ◦ **Saturn talisman** or bone-colored figure (goat, stairway, or mountain)
    ◦ **A single candle**: gray, black, or dark green
    ◦ **A coin or contract** (representing career or material responsibility)
3. Anoint altar edges with a **blend of CBD oil + vetiver**
4. Sit before it weekly to revisit goals, revise blueprints, and re-commit to long-term visions

Altar Invocation:
"I root into legacy. I rise with mastery. This space holds my oath to become."

Conclusion of Chapter 10

Capricorn and hemp converge at the intersection of **earthly ambition and spiritual structure**. Together, they teach the sacred value of slow mastery, sustainable creation, and lasting integrity. Hemp grounds Capricorn's mind, fuels its endurance, and honors its commitment to **building something that matters.**

Let this chapter serve as your **ritual infrastructure for greatness**. With each blend, smoke, intention, and altar, you become not only the worker—but the **weaver of your future temple**. Rise not in haste, but in *honor*.

Chapter 11 – Aquarius: The Visionary Bloom

Aquarius, the **revolutionary air sign of the zodiac**, is ruled by **Uranus**, the planet of **innovation, disruption, awakening, and progress**. Symbolized by the Water Bearer—who carries not water, but knowledge—Aquarius pours the future into the present, challenging norms and igniting evolution. This is the sign of the **visionary, rebel, genius, outsider, and collective healer**.

For Aquarius, hemp becomes a **bio-spiritual interface**—a plant not only for calm or healing, but for **channeling frequencies, decoding ideas, and activating neural clarity**. It is a sacred circuit, a botanical transmitter of intelligence and intuition, and a carrier of codes from higher realms.

This chapter explores how Aquarians—and those working with Aquarian energy—can use hemp to **access creative genius, stimulate social consciousness, integrate futuristic tech, and receive psychic downloads from the edge of what's known**.

Hemp and Future-Forward Thinking

Aquarius thrives on **abstract ideas, visionary inventions, and conceptual leaps**. But with so much mental electricity, it can often feel scattered, anxious, or dissociated from the body. Hemp acts as a **balancing circuit**—enhancing innovation while gently **grounding nervous system overstimulation**.

Hemp for Innovation Activation:

- Use a **sativa-dominant hemp strain or light CBD blend** to enhance mental sharpness
- Pair with **air element herbs** like lemongrass, blue lotus, and butterfly pea flower
- Brew before brainstorming, problem-solving, or creative planning

Aquarius Herbal Elixir for Visionary Focus:

- 1 tsp hemp flower
- ½ tsp butterfly pea flower (clarity + third eye stimulation)
- 1 tsp rosemary (mental energy)
- Pinch of gotu kola (cognition and memory)
- Optional: a drop of peppermint tincture

Drink during sunrise journaling or late-night conceptual downloads. Aquarius often receives insight **outside linear time**—this blend supports both reception and articulation.

Affirmation:

"I think in futures. I anchor what others fear to imagine."

Uranus-Aligned Creativity Boosts and Unconventional Rituals

Uranus governs **sudden insight, lightning flashes of genius, and technological evolution**. It also rules **ritual disruption**—Aquarius doesn't follow traditional paths. Their magic is unconventional, experimental, and often symbolic of collective shifts.

Uranian Creativity Boost:

1. Prepare a room with **hemp incense or a diffuser blend** of hemp oil + peppermint + neroli
2. Play **binaural beats or ambient frequencies**
3. Sit with a notebook or digital device and free-write on:
   - "What idea has been trying to find me?"
   - "What has never been done—but could be?"
   - "What do I want to invent for the collective?"
4. Draw symbols, maps, or mind-connections
5. End with a breath-focused hemp inhalation (dry herb vape or micro-smoke) and movement

For Aquarius, **ritual is never rote**—it's a **living algorithm**, constantly evolving.

Group Meditations Using Hemp for Collective Awakening

Aquarius is the **sign of the collective**. It governs global consciousness, social reform, and vibrational networks. Group meditations—especially when paired with hemp—can synchronize brainwaves, enhance empathic awareness, and catalyze **group-level awakening or intention-setting**.

Collective Hemp Meditation Protocol:

- Each participant consumes a **CBD microdose** or hemp-infused tea (CBD + lemon balm + lavender)
- Circle structure: seated or linked by stones/crystals
- Intention: "Awaken, align, and amplify the field"
- Use synchronized breathing: inhale for 4, hold for 4, exhale for 6
- Collective visualization:
  - Imagine a **light web** stretching between each participant
  - Feel the energy of **individual vision merging into shared purpose**

End by speaking into a **shared intention bowl** (hemp bowl or cauldron), then releasing the words through symbolic fire or breath.

Ideal Timing: New Moons in Aquarius, 11:11 portals, or Uranus transits.

Hemp and Crystal Tech: Pairing with Selenite and Amethyst

Aquarius energy is deeply **crystalline and electric**. Hemp, as a **plant fiber of conductivity**, pairs exquisitely with certain crystals to create energetic tools, devices, and wearable rituals.

Crystal Pairings:

- **Selenite + Hemp**: For channeling, clearing psychic fog, connecting to higher realms
- **Amethyst + Hemp**: For intuition, protection, and third eye opening
- **Herkimer Diamond + Hemp Cord**: For quantum dreaming and astral projection
- **Black Tourmaline + Hemp**: For grounding high-frequency downloads into practical form

Tech-Age Hemp Ritual:

- Wrap your selenite wand or amethyst cluster in **hemp cord**
- Anoint with **CBD oil + bergamot**
- Place on your altar beside your journal or near your digital devices
- Use during **digital detoxes, channeled writing, or stargazing sessions**

Aquarius Invocation:

"I connect above and below. I code the future with grace."

Hemp Codes and Downloads from Aquarian Portals
Aquarius is attuned to **starseed information, alien frequencies, cosmic maps, and etheric technology**. Hemp, when used in stillness, becomes a **tuning fork**—receiving "downloads" from multidimensional realms.

Portal Download Ritual (Solo):

1. Light a single white or violet candle
2. Drink a blend of **hemp, mugwort, and elderflower**
3. Lie flat with selenite on chest, amethyst on third eye
4. Play soft static, white noise, or a silent frequency app
5. Allow visuals, symbols, words, or feelings to arrive
6. Journal without analysis—these are **code fragments** to be interpreted later

Symbols may appear as:

- Glyphs
- Star patterns
- Spiral equations
- Color or tone flashes
- Nonlinear phrases or cosmic riddles

This ritual is best performed during:

- **Sun or Moon in Aquarius**
- **Mercury retrograde in air signs**
- **Eclipse portals or galactic center alignments**

Hemp in this context acts as a **dimensional translator**, helping Aquarians **receive, record, and reflect cosmic insight**.

Conclusion of Chapter 11

Aquarius and hemp co-create a **future-facing ritual ecosystem**—one that bridges spirit and science, solitude and society, the stars and the soil. With every breath, blend, crystal, and innovation, hemp helps Aquarius **transmit ideas that do not belong to this time—but are *needed* in it**.

Let this chapter be your invitation to **ritualize rebellion, meditate in networks, and bloom from the edge of what's known**. You are the visionary. Hemp is your signal amplifier. Together, you code the new age.

Chapter 12 – Pisces: The Mystic Vine

Pisces, the **dreamer and mystic of the zodiac**, is ruled by **Neptune**, planet of **illusion, intuition, dreams, divine love, and cosmic unity**. Represented by two fish swimming in opposite directions, Pisces is the threshold between the physical and spiritual realms. It is the sign of **visionaries, empaths, healers, artists, and seers**—those who dissolve ego to merge with the greater whole.

In the Piscean current, **hemp becomes a vine of the soul**, guiding the sensitive spirit gently through the depths of emotion, dream, creativity, and spiritual surrender. Hemp here isn't about grounding as much as it is about **flowing**—supporting Pisces to navigate their porous boundaries, magnify their gifts, and restore clarity after emotional overwhelm.

This chapter explores how Pisces can use hemp for **spiritual immersion, astral travel, emotional release, artistic transcendence, and energetic replenishment**. This is the realm where hemp becomes the **mystic vine**—twining around the soul like a sacred thread between heaven and water.

Hemp for Spiritual Depth, Dreams, and Divine Flow

Pisces lives with one foot in this world and one in the eternal. While this gives them access to profound insight, it also creates vulnerability to **emotional exhaustion, escapism, and energetic entanglement**. Hemp, when used with clear intention, offers **gentle containment and spiritual refinement**.

Divine Flow Hemp Elixir:

- **Hemp flower** (CBD-rich, calming)
- **Blue lotus** (Neptunian flower of visions and sacred union)
- **Passionflower** (emotional gentleness)
- **Spearmint** (clarity in fog)
- Optional: 1 drop rose oil (for heart activation)

Drink before **spiritual journaling, dream incubation, or meditation**. Pisces doesn't need sharp focus—they need a **softened awareness** that allows impressions and images to rise like mist.

Affirmation:
"I flow in divine rhythm. I dream awake. I receive without resistance."

Neptune-Infused Rituals for Astral Journeying

Neptune governs **altered states, trance, imagination, astral projection, and spiritual surrender**. Pisces, as Neptune's child, can naturally leave the body, whether through dreams, deep meditation, or even emotional merging with others. Hemp enhances this process when used with **intentional breathwork and protective ritual design**.

Astral Travel Ritual:

1. Dim the lights. Light a **blue or violet candle**
2. Inhale a **ritual smoke blend** of:
   ◦ Hemp flower
   ◦ Mugwort (dreaming and astral work)
   ◦ Damiana (opens sensual connection to spirit)
   ◦ Lavender (calm entry into altered states)
3. Lie flat. Place a **moonstone** or **amethyst** on the third eye
4. Speak:
   "I surrender to the current of stars. Guide me gently."
5. Visualize yourself floating upward through a tunnel of soft light
6. Allow impressions, guides, or symbols to appear

Always close with **saltwater hand-washing or grounding breath**, as Pisces must gently **return to the body** to avoid soul drift.

Water + Hemp Rituals for Emotional Clearing

Pisces is a **water sign**—and water is not just emotional but **ritualistic**. It holds memory, absorbs intention, and responds to vibration. When paired with hemp, water becomes a sacred clearing agent—washing away fear, sorrow, confusion, or psychic residue.

Emotional Clearing Bath:

- Fill a tub with:
    - 1 cup **hemp milk** or hemp oil
    - ½ cup **sea salt**
    - 1 tsp **dried jasmine or yarrow**
    - 3 drops **sandalwood or neroli oil**
- Light floating candles or blue LEDs
- Play gentle soundscapes (harp, chimes, ocean waves)
- Enter the bath and repeat:

  "All I carry that is not mine, I release with love. I am light in water."

Visualize cords, shadows, and fog dissolving into the water. Drain with gratitude.

Dream Recall and Protection with Hemp Sachets

Pisces receives **downloads through dreams**, but their empathic openness makes them susceptible to **night terrors, entity intrusion, or emotional bleed-through**. Hemp sachets act as both **anchors and guardians** in the dream realm.

Dream Sachet for Protection & Recall:

- 1 tsp **dried hemp flower**
- Pinch of **mugwort** (for vivid dreams)
- **Chamomile or lemon balm** (to soothe)
- 1 small **amethyst or lepidolite chip**
- A hand-written sigil or phrase for protection:
  "Only truth may enter. I sleep in clarity."

Sew into a light-blue pouch. Place beneath the pillow or hang over the bed. Cleanse regularly with **moonlight and hemp smoke**.

For enhanced recall, **journal immediately upon waking**, capturing:

- Symbols
- Emotions
- Colors
- Phrases heard
- Visited places

Pisces dreams are **prophetic and poetic**—treat them like sacred texts.

Hemp for Artistic Channeling and Etheric Expression

Pisces is the **artist of the soul**—expressing what words can't capture. Music, painting, dance, poetry, and even spiritual conversation become channels for Pisces to **transmit energy from unseen realms**. Hemp softens the ego barrier so that Pisces may fully **embody the muse**.

Artistic Channeling Ritual:

1. Inhale a **sacred hemp blend** (hemp + rose + blue lotus)
2. Sit with your chosen medium—instrument, brush, voice recorder, canvas
3. Light incense (frankincense + hemp oil) and speak:
   "I offer my vessel to the divine. Flow through me."
4. Begin creating without planning. Let emotion, color, sound, or rhythm lead
5. Afterward, close with gentle grounding: hold black tourmaline or hematite, drink warm ginger tea

Pisces' challenge is to **remain whole while channeling the whole**. Hemp offers that **container of calm**, allowing creativity to bloom without loss of self.

Conclusion of Chapter 12

Pisces and hemp are **natural allies of mysticism**. Together, they weave a sanctuary of dreams, spiritual wisdom, emotional beauty, and divine flow. Hemp is the **vine that curls through the veil**, offering support as Pisces dives into the ocean of consciousness—and returns bearing gifts of compassion, art, and healing.

Let this final chapter be your invitation to **remember the sacredness of your sensitivity**, the power of your imagination, and the wisdom in your emotions. Through hemp, water, dream, and ether—Pisces doesn't escape the world. It **softens it with grace**.

Appendix A – Cosmic Hemp Reference Chart

Astro-Hemp Alignment for Ritual, Healing, and Magick

This chart is designed as a **quick-access cosmic alignment tool** to help you integrate **hemp with your zodiac sign's elemental energy, planetary ruler, and ritual strengths**. Whether you're crafting a blend, designing a spell, or planning a wellness session, use this chart to guide your choices for optimal spiritual, physical, and emotional synergy.

Zodiac Sign	Hemp Strain Type	Element	Planetary Ruler	Best Ritual Timing	Ideal Consumption	Herb Pairing	Crystal Pairing	Chakra
Aries	Sativa-leaning Hybrid	Fire	Mars	Waxing Moon, Tuesdays, Mars hour	Smoke or topical oil	Ginger root	Carnelian	Solar Plexus (3rd)
Taurus	CBD-Dominant Indica	Earth	Venus	Fridays, Taurus Moon, Venus transits	Edibles or infused bath	Rose petals	Rose Quartz	Heart (4th)
Gemini	Sativa or Balanced	Air	Mercury	Mercury hour, Gemini Moon, Waning Moon	Tea or vapor	Peppermint	Blue Lace Agate	Throat (5th)
Cancer	Indica/CBD-Rich	Water	Moon	New Moon, Full Moon in Cancer, Moon hour	Bath or tea	Chamomile	Moonstone	Sacral (2nd)
Leo	Sativa or CBD Hybrid	Fire	Sun	Noon, Sunday, Leo Moon, Solar Return	Tincture or oil rub	Cinnamon	Citrine	Solar Plexus (3rd)

| **Virgo** | Balanced CBD Hybrid | Earth | Mercury | New Moon, Virgo Moon, Mercury hour | Tea or capsule | Fennel seed | Moss Agate | Root (1st) |

| **Libra** | CBD-Dominant | Air | Venus | Libra Moon, Venus hour, Equinoxes | Oil, tea, or incense | Lavender | Amethyst | Heart (4th) |

| **Scorpio** | Indica | Water | Pluto (Modern) / Mars (Traditional) | Scorpio Moon, Full Moon, Eclipse portals | Smoke or ritual incense | Mugwort | Obsidian | Sacral (2nd) |

| **Sagittarius** | Sativa | Fire | Jupiter | Jupiter hour, Sagittarius Moon, Full Moon | Tea or travel talisman | Lemongrass | Lapis Lazuli | Crown (7th) |

| **Capricorn** | CBD-Heavy Hybrid | Earth | Saturn | New Moon, Capricorn Moon, Saturn day/hour | Tincture or grounded smoke | Vetiver | Black Tourmaline | Root (1st) |

| **Aquarius** | Sativa-leaning Hybrid | Air | Uranus | Aquarius Moon, Uranus transits, 11:11 portals | Vape or elixir | Butterfly Pea | Selenite | Third Eye (6th) |

| **Pisces** | Indica or CBD Dominant| Water | Neptune | Pisces Moon, Dream hours (early AM), Neptune transits | Tea or bath | Blue Lotus | Amethyst | Crown (7th) |

Key Usage Notes:

- **Hemp Strain Type** is based on the sign's elemental needs and energetic tendencies. Fire signs thrive with uplifting Sativas, while Earth and Water signs often need grounding Indicas or high-CBD options.

- **Ritual Timing** maximizes planetary alignment for manifestation, healing, or energetic clarity. Use a planetary hours calculator or moon calendar to sync accurately.

- **Consumption Method** is curated for each sign's lifestyle and energy expression. Air signs benefit from inhalation rituals; Earth signs thrive with infused products; Water signs with immersion; Fire signs with activating applications.

- **Herb Pairing** amplifies hemp's properties and aligns with planetary and elemental influences.
- **Crystal Pairing** enhances vibrational harmony for ritual, dreamwork, protection, or expansion.
- **Chakra** focuses your ritual intention and bodily awareness.

<u>Message from the Author:</u>

I hope you enjoyed this book, I love astrology and knew there was not a book such as this out on the shelf. I love metaphysical items as well. Please check out my other books:

-Life of Government Benefits

-My life of Hell

-My life with Hydrocephalus

-Red Sky

-World Domination:Woman's rule

-World Domination:Woman's Rule 2: The War

-Life and Banishment of Apophis: book 1

-The Kidney Friendly Diet

-The Ultimate Hemp Cookbook

-Creating a Dispensary(legally)

-Cleanliness throughout life: the importance of showering from childhood to adulthood.

-Strong Roots: The Risks of Overcoddling children

-Hemp Horoscopes: Cosmic Insights and Earthly Healing

- Celestial Hemp Navigating the Zodiac: Through the Green Cosmos

-Astrological Hemp: Aligning The Stars with Earth's Ancient Herb

-The Astrological Guide to Hemp: Stars, Signs, and Sacred Leaves

-Green Growth: Innovative Marketing Strategies for your Hemp Products and Dispensary

-Cosmic Cannabis

-Astrological Munchies

-Henry The Hemp

-Zodiacal Roots: The Astrological Soul Of Hemp

- **Green Constellations: Intersection of Hemp and Zodiac**

-Hemp in The Houses: An astrological Adventure Through The Cannabis Galaxy

-Galactic Ganja Guide

Heavenly Hemp

Zodiac Leaves

Doctor Who Astrology

Cannastrology

Stellar Satvias and Cosmic Indicas

Celestial Cannabis: A Zodiac Journey

AstroHerbology: The Sky and The Soil: Volume 1

AstroHerbology:Celestial Cannabis:Volume 2

Cosmic Cannabis Cultivation

The Starry Guide to Herbal Harmony: Volume 1

The Starry Guide to Herbal Harmony: Cannabis Universe: Volume 2

Yugioh Astrology: Astrological Guide to Deck, Duels and more

Nightmare Mansion: Echoes of The Abyss

Nightmare Mansion 2: Legacy of Shadows

Nightmare Mansion 3: Shadows of the Forgotten

Nightmare Mansion 4: Echoes of the Damned

The Life and Banishment of Apophis: Book 2

Nightmare Mansion: Halls of Despair

Healing with Herb: Cannabis and Hydrocephalus

Planetary Pot: Aligning with Astrological Herbs: Volume 1

Fast Track to Freedom: 30 Days to Financial Independence Using AI, Assets, and Agile Hustles

Cosmic Hemp Pathways

How to Become Financially Free in 30 Days: 10,000 Paths to Prosperity

Zodiacal Herbage: Astrological Insights: Volume 1

Nightmare Mansion: Whispers in the Walls

The Daleks Invade Atlantis

Henry the hemp and Hydrocephalus

10X The Kidney Friendly Diet
Cannabis Universe: Adult coloring book
Hemp Astrology: The Healing Power of the Stars
Zodiacal Herbage: Astrological Insights: Cannabis Universe: Volume 2
<u>Planetary Pot: Aligning with Astrological Herbs: Cannabis Universes: Volume 2</u>
Doctor Who Meets the Replicators and SG-1: The Ultimate Battle for Survival
Nightmare Mansion: Curse of the Blood Moon
<u>The Celestial Stoner: A Guide to the Zodiac</u>
Cosmic Pleasures: Sex Toy Astrology for Every Sign
Hydrocephalus Astrology: Navigating the Stars and Healing Waters
Lapis and the Mischievous Chocolate Bar

Celestial Positions: Sexual Astrology for Every Sign
Apophis's Shadow Work Journal: **:** A Journey of Self-Discovery and Healing
Kinky Cosmos: Sexual Kink Astrology for Every Sign
Digital Cosmos: The Astrological Digimon Compendium
Stellar Seeds: The Cosmic Guide to Growing with Astrology
Apophis's Daily Gratitude Journal

Cat Astrology: Feline Mysteries of the Cosmos
The Cosmic Kama Sutra: An Astrological Guide to Sexual Positions
Unleash Your Potential: A Guided Journal Powered by AI Insights
Whispers of the Enchanted Grove

Cosmic Pleasures: An Astrological Guide to Sexual Kinks
369, 12 Manifestation Journal

Whisper of the nocturne journal(blank journal for writing or drawing)

The Boogey Book

Locked In Reflection: A Chastity Journey Through Locktober

Generating Wealth Quickly:How to Generate $100,000 in 24 Hours

Star Magic: Harness the Power of the Universe

The Flatulence Chronicles: A Fart Journal for Self-Discovery

The Doctor and The Death Moth

Seize the Day: A Personal Seizure Tracking Journal

The Ultimate Boogeyman Safari: A Journey into the Boogie World and Beyond

Whispers of Samhain: 1,000 Spells of Love, Luck, and Lunar Magic: Samhain Spell Book

Apophis's guides:Witch's Spellbook Crafting Guide for Halloween

<u>Frost & Flame: The Enchanted Yule Grimoire of 1000 Winter Spells</u>

<u>The Ultimate Boogey Goo Guide & Spooky Activities for Halloween Fun</u>

Harmony of the Scales: A Libra's Spellcraft for Balance and Beauty

The Enchanted Advent: 36 Days of Christmas Wonders

Nightmare Mansion: The Labyrinth of Screams

Harvest of Enchantment: 1,000 Spells of Gratitude, Love, and Fortune for Thanksgiving

The Boogey Chronicles: A Journal of Nightly Encounters and Shadowy Secrets

The 12 Days of Financial Freedom: A Step-by-Step Christmas Countdown to Transform Your Finances

Sigil of the Eternal Spiral Blank Journal

A Christmas Feast: Timeless Recipes for Every Meal

Holiday Stress-Free Solutions: A Survival Guide to Thriving During the Festive Season

Whispers of the Harvest: The Corn Mother's Journal

The Evergreen Spellbook

The Doctor Meets the Boogeyman

The White Witch of Rose Hall's SpellBook

The Gingerbread Golem's Shadow: A Study in Sweet Darkness

The Gingerbread Golem Codex: An Academic Exploration of Sweet Myths

The Gingerbread Golem Grimoire: Sweet Magicks and Spells for the Festive Witch

The Curse of the Gingerbread Golem

10-minute Christmas Crafts for kids

<u>**Christmas Crisis Solutions: The Ultimate Last-Minute Survival Guide**</u>

Gingerbread Golem Recipes: Holiday Treats with a Magical Twist

The Infinite Key: Unlocking Mystical Secrets of the Ages

Enchanted Yule: A Wiccan and Pagan Guide to a Magical and Memorable Season

Dinosaurs of Power: Unlocking Ancient Magick

Astro-Dinos: The Cosmic Guide to Prehistoric Wisdom

Gallifrey's Yule Logs: A Festive Doctor Who Cookbook

The Dino Grimoire: Secrets of Prehistoric Magick

The Gift They Never Knew They Needed

The Gingerbread Golem's Culinary Alchemy: Enchanting Recipes for a Sweetly Dark Feast

A Time Lord Christmas: Holiday Adventures with the Doctor

Krampusproofing Your Home: Defensive Strategies for Yule

Silent Frights: A Collection of Christmas Creepypastas to Chill Your Bones

Santa Raptor's Jolly Carnage: A Dino-Claus Christmas Tale

Prehistoric Palettes: A Dino Wicca Coloring Journey

The Christmas Wishkeeper Chronicles

The Starlight Sleigh: A Holiday Journey

Elf Secrets: The True Magic of the North Pole

Six More Weeks: Embracing Seasonal Transitions
The Lumivian Chronicles: Fragments of the Fifth Dimension
Money on Your Mind: A Beginner's Guide to Wealth
The Focus Fix: Breaking Through Distraction
January's Spirit Keepers: Mystical Protectors of the Cold
Creativity Unchained: Unlocking Your Wildest Ideas in 2025
Manifestation Mastery: 365 Days to Rewrite Your Reality
The Groundhog's Mirror: Reflecting on Change
The Weeping Angels' Christmas Curse
Burrowed in Time: A Groundhog Day Journey
Heartbeats: Poems to Share with Your Valentine
Dino Wicca: The Sacred Grimoire of Prehistoric Magick
Courage of the Pride: Finding Your Inner Roar
The Lion's Leap: Bold Moves for Big Results
Healthy Hustle: Achieving Without Overworking
Practical Manifesting: Turning Dreams into Reality in 2025
Jurassic Pharaohs: Unlocking the Magick of Ancient Egypt and Dino Wicca
The Happiness Equation: Small Changes for Big Joy
The Confidence Compass: Finding Your Inner Strength
Whispers in the Hollow: Tales of the Forgotten Beasts
Echoes from the Hollow: The Return of Forgotten Beasts
The Hollow Ascendant: The Rise of the Forgotten Beasts
The Relationship Reset: Building Better Connections
Mastering the Morning: How to Win the Day Before 8 AM
The Shadow's Dance: Groundhog Day Symbolism
Cupid's Kitchen: Quick Valentine's Day Recipes
Valentine's Day on a Budget: Love Without Breaking the Bank
Astrocraft: Aligning the Stars in the World of Minecraft
Forecasting Life: Groundhog Day Reflections
Bleeding Hearts: Twisted Tales of Valentine's Terror
Herbal Smoke Revolution: The Ultimate Guide to Nature's Cigarette Alternative

Winter's Wrath: The Complete Survival Blueprint for Extreme Freezes.

The Groundhog's Shadow: A Tale of Seasons
Burrowed Insights: Wisdom from the Groundhog
Sensual Strings: The Art of Erotic Bondage
Whispered Flames: Unlocking the Power of Fire Play
Forgotten Shadows: A Guide to Cryptids Lost to Time
Six Weeks of Secrets: Groundhog Day's Hidden Messages
Shadows and Cycles: Groundhog Day Reflections
The Art of Love Letters: Crafting the Perfect Message
Romantic Getaways at Home: Turning Your Space into Paradise
Purrfect Brews: A Cat Lover's Guide to Coffee and Companionship
The Groundhog's Wisdom: Timeless Lessons for Modern Life
The Shadow Oracle: Groundhog Day as a Predictor
Emerging from the Burrow: A Journey of Renewal
The Language of Love: Learning Your Partner's Love Style
Authorpreneur: The Ultimate Blueprint for Writing, Publishing, and Thriving as an Author
Weathering the Seasons: Groundhog Day Perspectives
Valentine's Day Magic: A Guide to Romantic Rituals
The Shadow Chronicles: Stories of Groundhog Day
Love and Laughter: Fun Games for Valentine's Day
AstroRealty: Unlocking the Stars for Property Success
The Groundhog's Path: A Guide to Seasonal Balance
Groundhog Day Diaries: Reflections in the Shadow
The Groundhog's Light: Illuminating the Path Ahead
Valentine's Traditions from Around the World
AI Wealth Revolution: Unlocking the Trillionaire Mindset
Love Rekindled: Reigniting Passion in Relationships
Single and Thriving: Self-Love on Valentine's Day
Emerald Legends: Mystical Tales of Ireland

Green Alchemy: Harnessing Nature's Magic

The Hearts of Horror: A Valentine's Day Nightmare

The Leprechaun's Guide to Wealth and Wisdom

Dancing with the Sidhe: Celebrating the Otherworld

Shamrocks and Shadows: Mysteries of the Green Isle

Emerald Energy: Harnessing Luck and Growth

The Gingerbread Golem's Valentine: A Sweetheart's Guide to Love and Enchantment

The Celtic Knot: Weaving Life and Destiny

Green Fire: Elemental Magic for St. Patrick's Day

Clover Chronicles: Finding Your Inner Luck

Ireland's Mystical Creatures: A Field Guide

Gingerbread Golem's Love Almanac

Prowl and Thrive: The Lion's Guide to Success

Love Alchemy: Transforming Your Life Through Heart Energy

WORLD DOMINATION: Woman's Rule 3:The New Life

The Midnight Rose: A Guide to Lunar Love Spells

The Forbidden Letters: Writing Your Own Love Prophecy

Luck and Lore: St. Patrick's Day for Modern Mystics

The Green Path: A Pagan Celebration of Renewal

The Dark Architect's Guide to Reprogramming Reality

Prankster's Paradise: A Guide to Harmless Hijinks

Manifest Your Reality: The Law of Attraction Simplified

The TARDIS Owner's Manual: Understanding the Doctor's Ship: *A complete guide to the TARDIS, its technology, secrets, and mysteries*

Starlit Romance: Astrology Secrets for Finding True Love

The Time Lord's Atlas: A Complete Guide to the Whoniverse: *A breakdown of the locations, planets, and dimensions explored in Doctor Who*

Sweetheart Shadows: The Dark Side of Love and Attraction

February Fire: Reigniting Passion in Every Area of Life

The Witch's Guide to Parenting: Raising Empowered and Intuitive Children

The Magick of Motherhood: Reclaiming Your Power Through Rituals

The Pagan Path to Self-Love: A Goddess's Guide to Worth and Confidence

Wild Woman Magick: Unleashing Your Primal Power

The Money Magnet Blueprint: Unlocking Unlimited Wealth

Biohacking 101: Unlock Your Body's Full Potential

The Wild Father: A Pagan Guide to Strength and Wisdom

The Sacred Masculine: Unlocking Your Inner Power

The Druid's Compass

The Warrior's Mindset

The Father's Fire

Odin's Path

Ancestral Bonds

The House That Whispers

The Magician's Code

The Wild Hunt

The Green Man's Path

The Altar of Success

The Shadow and the Sword

The High Priestess's Guide to Energy Healing

The Lunar Mother

The Sacred Self-Care Grimoire

The Womb Wisdom Codex

The Wheel of the Mother

The Witch's Guide to Manifestation

The Q2 Reset

The Ultimate Guide to AI-Powered Passive Income

Escape the 9-5

AI Feline Fortunes

The Tear-Stained Grimoire

Razorblade Runes
Cemetery Sirens
The Midnight Wristwatch
The Town That Forgets
AI Horror & Creepypasta
The Hollow Frequency
The Breach Echo
The Quiet Between Worlds
The Sigil of Tharan-Khul
Summon the Vault of Y'ha'ten
The Becoming Codex
The Profit of Az'ra-nar
The Drowned Logos
Echoes of the Eldritch Will
The Deep Ledger
Necronomicon of Networth
Covenant of the Wealthwyrm
The Whisperer's Manifesto
The Rites of Azh-K'luth
The Ark of the Crawling Coin
The Tithe of Shadows
Inkheart Abyss
The Timewinds of Y'ha-nthlei
The Spiral Labyrinth of Azag-Nirrh
The Gallifreyan Heresy of the Black Pharaoh
The Psalms of Nyog-Sotha
Black Rain Alchemy
The Infinite Maw
The Entropic Blueprint
The Oracle of Sh'guul
The Book of Breach
The Drowned Saint's Testament
Dreamcraft of the Sleeper God

The Silence Market

Cthonomics: The Dark Wealth Algorithm

Invocation of the Ten-Eyed King

Wealthbound to the Wyrm Below

Become the Unnameable

Codex of the Sovereign Flame

Rituals of Relentless Becoming

The Shadow Ascends

The Eyes Beneath You

The Will That Wakes Worlds

Silence Is a Weapon

The Mirror That Screams

The Whisper Between Moments

The Mind That Devours Fear

The Myth of the Finished Self

The Architect of Your Madness

The Voice You've Buried

The Discipline of Madness

Stormborn: Awakening Your Inner Tempest

The Mind That Ate Time

Unbind Your Becoming

The Pact You Owe Yourself

The Devourer's Diet

The Acid That Carves the Path

The Tower You Must Burn

The Breath Between Worlds

Speak Like the Deep

The Labyrinth Within

The Spine of the Sea God

Rejection Is a Portal

The Crown You Refused

The Scar Is the Spell

The Lightless Flame

The Habit of Becoming Horrific

ChickenJockey Chaos

The Gatekeeper Within

You Are Not Your Name

The Compass of the Mad

The Archive of Unsent Letters

What the Mirror Can't Show You

The Knife You Needed

Worship Nothing, Become Everything

The Other Voice

The Body the World Forgot

The Vein of the Void

The Black Bone Codex

The Puzzle of the Hidden Self (Millennium Puzzle)

The Eye That Sees the Lie *(Millennium Eye)*

The Ring of Return (Millennium Ring)

The Rod of Relentless Will *(Millennium Rod)*

The Tally of the Soul (Millennium Tauk/Necklace)

The Key to the Locked Timeline (Millennium Key)

The Scale of Sacred Decisions (Millennium Scales)

Inferno Bites: The UnOfficial Minecraft Lava Cookbook

Rot in the Attic

Prana: The Hidden Force of Your Infinite Self

The Shadow Realm Within: Transforming Darkness Into Destiny

The Borderland Collapse

Claws of Protection: Bastet's Defensive Magick

Mr. Ring-a-Ding's Madness

Yugioh Astrology: Celestial Deckcraft and Duel Destiny (2026–2027 Edition)

The Seal You Signed: Unlocking the Power You Once Feared

The Puzzle of Infinite Minds: Unlocking the Mentalism Hidden Within

Harnessed Minds: Breaking Free from Mental Control

The Eyes in the Smoke

Rootwake: The Carbon Covenant

Skitter Logic: Unlearning the Fear That Built You

Doctor Who: The World That Froths

Rootwake: The Fizz That Rewrites Flesh

Rootwake: Frothfather of the World

The Holly Pact: Blood Beneath the Mistletoe

The 2nd Mass Principle: Building Unbreakable Tribes

Web of Wits: A Survival Guide to Encounters with Anasi the Spider (Aunt Nancy)

The Hexbreaking Handbook: Effective Spells to Remove Curses

Pop Alchemy: Transform Your Life One Sip at a Time

The Mason Code: Leading in Unleadable Times

Petosiris and the Fifth Chamber of Thoth

The Ether Seed Within

The Parent of Tomorrow

Petosiris's Pyramid of Perpetual Wealth

Unlearn the World

Grimoire of the Hollow Tongue

Zodiac Weeds: Finding Your Strain Through the Stars

Aquarius Rises in the Bank

The Sugar God's Smile

The Skinclock Reversal: Biohacking the Face of Time

Debtburn: How to Obliterate What You Owe Forever

The Ice Cream Oracle: What Your Cone Says About Your Future

Silence Is Sovereignty: The Power of Being Unreadable

The Wind That Whispers Through Stone

Path of the Four Directions

Doctor Who: The Maestro's Symphony of Endings

Oxygen Grail: Breathing to Undo the Clock

Zodiacal Collapse: When Stars Devour Time
Teachings from the Red Sand Silence

Get Some Tarot cards: https://www.makeplayingcards.com/sell/apophis-occult-shop

<u>Get some shirts: https://www.bonfire.com/store/apophis-shirt-emporium/</u>

Instagrams:
@apophis_enterprises,
@apophisbookemporium,
@apophisscardshop
Twitter: @apophisenterpr1
Tiktok:@apophisenterprise
Youtube: @sg1fan23477
Hive: @sg1fan23477
CheeLee: @SG1fan23477

Podcast: Apophis Chat Zone: https://open.spotify.com/show/5zXbrCLEV2xzCp8ybrfHsk?si=fb4d4fdbdce44dec

Newsletter: https://apophiss-newsletter-27c897.beehiiv.com/

If you want to support me or see posts of other projects that I have come over to: **buymeacoffee.com/mpetchinskg**
I post there daily several times a day

Get your Dinowicca or Christmas themed digital products, especially Santa Raptor songs and other musics. Here: **https://sg1fan23477.gumroad.com**

Apophis Yuletide Digital has not only digital Christmas items, but it will have all things with Dinowicca as well as other Digital products.